S0-BVN-938

forever sisters

by Jennifer Fujita

Copyright © 2009 Hallmark Licensing, Inc.

Published by Hallmark Books,
a division of Hallmark Cards, Inc.,
Kansas City, MO 64141
Visit us on the Web at www.Hallmark.com.

All rights reserved. No part of this publication may be reproduced, transmitted, or stored
in any form or by any means without the prior written permission of the publisher.

Editorial Director: Todd Hafer
Editor: Theresa Trinder
Art Director: Kevin Swanson
Designer: Sarah Smitka — The Pink Pear Design Co.
Production Artist: Dan C. Horton

ISBN: 978-1-59530-190-1

BOK4354

Printed and bound in China

forever sisters

by Jennifer Fujita

GIFT BOOKS
from Hallmark

Your sister.

Making faces behind you in family photographs. Shaking you awake on Saturday mornings. Sharing a knowing look when Mom says that thing she always says. Inside almost every childhood memory, there she is.

Without knowing it, in fact, sometimes without even liking it, the two of you formed a powerful, permanent bond created from thousands of tiny, seemingly forgettable moments. But who could ever forget? You'll always remember the little girls inside the women you are today. You'll always have a partner, a secret-keeper, a sidekick, and a friend. You'll always have someone to belong to.

And that is the miracle of sisterhood.

Then . . .

As close as you may have been, growing up together wasn't always easy.
Sometimes it seemed there was no space or time or attention that wasn't
somehow also hers. Whether by choice or under protest, you shared, split,
and divided everything until it became so ingrained that, to this day, you
still find yourself doing something like slipping your extra pickle onto her
plate, because, well . . . you always have.

Sisters understand the importance of communication.
This comes from years of trying to keep their stories straight
for Mom and Dad.

Because if you're going to break a house rule,
it's best to break it together.

Beware of sisters who have joined forces
against a common enemy.

No matter what the scheme, you can always count her in.

With a little teamwork, you can get Dad to believe

that taking you out for ice cream

was actually his idea.

Whether it involves gum or fire or mayonnaise,
behind every set of sisters is a hair-related tragedy
that lives on in family legend.

She's the one who taught you
that it's better to ask Mom for forgiveness
than for permission.

And that it's physically impossible
        not to roll your eyes
    when someone starts talking about
        "unladylike behavior" and "acting your age."

Be nice to your sister. She has pictures of you
from middle school . . .

and she has Internet access.

Sisters remember.
Not even an elephant has a memory like a sister
who was once tricked into eating a bug.

The definition of cooperation is cramming

a mountain of hair products, a hair dryer, a ton of makeup,

a curling iron, a CD player, and a couple of sisters

into a tiny bathroom with one outlet and one mirror.

And whoever said "a sister is a sheltering tree" clearly never had to fight for her share of the umbrella.

A sister is a rock.

But sometimes she's a big rock
blocking your view of the TV.

Sisters Rule 1: A hiding place, however creative,

is only as good as the company.

Sisters Rule 2: If she has been driving the car,
the gas tank will be close to empty.

Sisters Rule 3: Being forced to make up after a fight
is good practice for life.

Now . . .

You got in her stuff. She got in your face. And it seemed
like you were always getting each other in trouble.
You wouldn't have guessed it years ago while she was
yelling at you through the bathroom door, but there's
so much comfort in having someone in your life who
laughs at your jokes, who accepts your quirks without
trying to change them. Someone who holds your heart when
the chips are down and holds your hand when life looks up.

Someone who believes in you.
Someone to believe in.

Sharing might be optional for some people,
but for sisters, it's mandatory.

She's like a therapist.

A therapist who will give you a sweater,
half her dessert, and a ride to the airport. For free.

When you're with your sister, you are never, ever
required to fake a laugh. It's just not right.

Things your sister will always remind you about:

Mom's birthday.

Your share of Mom's birthday present.

That she still hasn't told Mom it was really you who broke the garbage disposal.

She will *always* cover for you . . . for a price.

Sisters' minds think alike. As in,

"Forget the gym . . . let's get pedicures."

Because you're not just sisters.
You're friends who are so similar,
it's creepy.

Three in the afternoon,

three in the morning . . .

there's never a bad time

to call your sister.

You should be grateful for all the things
your sister has given you. Except chickenpox,
whooping cough, poison ivy, or lice.
You probably could have done without those things.

Your sister shares in the victory
when you finally find the perfect bra.

A sister is a faithful companion on the road of life.

That's why she's always telling you how to drive.

And she's the best gift your parents ever gave you.

Especially if they never gave you a car.

Forever . . .

You can see it—that your ideas about love and loyalty have
been formed by each other. You've been one another's teacher,
mirror, and friend. And deep down, you understand what only
sisters can know: That you belong to each other in a way that
you can never belong to anyone else. That a love that grows
through stages and phases is stronger for having been tested
time and time again. That sticking together works—and
that you've pressed forward, shoulder to shoulder, past every
curveball life has thrown at you.

And you always will.

Going through life with the family thighs is hard.
But it's a lot easier when there's somebody else
with two more just like them.

When you're telling a sister a story, you can skip
all the background info and start right at the good part.
This saves A LOT of time.

You can talk your sister into going with you
to that movie, concert, museum, craft show, street fair,
or rummage sale nobody else is ever interested in.

You can always ask her which fork to use at a fancy restaurant. She might not know . . . but you can always ask her.

When it comes to brutal honesty,

sisters are almost as good as

those three-way dressing room mirrors.

You'll never be in doubt about whether
    you've overaccessorized, need a haircut,
or have something in your teeth.

Being the younger sister is no fun . . .

until you're past thirty.

Then it's fun to tell EVERYONE.

When she's feeling generous,
            your sister may still sometimes
    let you boss her around.

Having a sister means there's always at least one person who'll buy stuff for your kids' school fundraisers.

If you don't feel like talking,
your sister doesn't automatically assume you're mad at her.
And when you do feel like talking,
she'll drop everything and listen.

And you'll do the same.

About the Author

Jennifer Fujita is a writer for Hallmark Cards and the
middle of three sisters who still wear each other's clothes,
finish each other's sentences, and share an unfortunate
amount of dessert during their annual "Sisters Summit."

If you have enjoyed this book
or it has touched your life in some way,
we would love to hear from you.

Please send your comments to:
Hallmark Book Feedback
P.O. Box 419034
Mail Drop 215
Kansas City, MO 64141

Or e-mail us at:
booknotes@hallmark.com